The Real Thing

Iris Howden

Published in association with
The Basic Skills Agency

Hodder & Stoughton

Acknowledgements
Illustrations: Juan Hayward.
Cover: Ben Warner/Organisation.

Orders: please contact Bookpoint Ltd, 39 Milton Park, Abingdon, Oxon OX14
4TD. Telephone: (44) 01235 400414, Fax: (44) 01235 400454. Lines are open
from 9.00–6.00, Monday to Saturday, with a 24 hour message answering service.
Email address: orders@bookpoint.co.uk

A CIP record is available from the British Library

ISBN 0 340 72092 1

First published 1998
New edition 1998
Impression number   10 9 8 7 6 5 4 3
Year   2002 2001 2000 1999

Copyright © 1998 Iris Howden

Typeset by Fakenham Photosetting Ltd, Fakenham, Norfolk.
Printed in Great Britain for Hodder & Stoughton Educational, a division of
Hodder Headline Plc, 338 Euston Road, London NW1 3BH by Athenaeum Press
Ltd, Gateshead, Tyne & Wear.

The Real Thing

Contents

1

A New Job

Vicky ran across the road.
She got into Tony's car. They kissed.
'You're late,' Tony said.
'I know. I couldn't help it.
A woman came in at ten-to-five.
She asked for a cut and blow-dry.

But I love working at HAIR BY JAY'S.
It's much better than Brenda's shop was.'

Tony drove as Vicky talked.
She talked about her new job.
She told Tony about her boss, Jay,
how classy the shop was.
How smart the clients were.
How nice the other girls had been.
'It's great,' she said. 'Working with people
of my own age.
And the work's more fun.
I'm trying out some new styles.
It's a change from doing perms
for old ladies.'
'You used to like Brenda's shop,' Tony said.
'And it was near to home.
The traffic in the city is murder.'

'Oh well, if it's too much trouble
giving me a lift,' Vicky said.
'I can always get the bus.'
'It's not that,' Tony told her.
'It's just that we haven't got long.
I thought we'd grab a bite to eat.
I have to be back at work by seven.'

'You're not working late again!'
Vicky sounded cross.
'That's the third time this week.'
'I can't turn down the overtime,' Tony said.
'The boss might not ask me again.'
Tony was a shop fitter.
A lot of his work was done after closing time.

They drove up the main street
past the theatre.

'I see your hero's on at the Grand,'
Tony said.
'He's not my hero,' Vicky said.
But she felt her face go red.
It was true.
She really liked Drew Denton.
It was such a pity he'd left *Ward 7*.
That was the best soap on TV.
It wasn't the same since he'd left the show.
'Guess what?' she asked Tony.
'Jay says a lot of the stars come in to
our shop. I might end up doing Drew's hair.'

'Big deal,' Tony said. 'Maybe if you get
to meet the real thing you won't try
and turn me into a Drew look-alike.'
Vicky blushed again.

She had tried to change Tony.
She wanted him to have high-lights
in his hair, like Drew.

She looked at Tony now.
He was like Drew Denton in some ways,
she thought.

2

Meeting Drew

'It's him. It's Drew Denton.'
The words went round the shop.
Women turned to look as he came in.
Vicky felt her legs go weak.
Drew was here – in the flesh.
Jay waved a hand at the girl on the desk.
Drew would be seen to right away.

One of the girls took Drew's jacket.
She hung it up.
Vicky watched her.
The jacket was cream.
It looked expensive.
She took note of his silk shirt.
She looked at his gold watch,
his deep sun tan.
Vicky found it hard to keep her mind
on her customer's blow-dry.
Mandy was washing Drew's hair.
Vicky looked at him in the mirror.

Then Jay's voice cut across the salon.
'Vicky, can you do Mr Denton's cut next?'
As if in a dream she saw Drew
coming towards her.
He sat down in the black leather chair.

Vicky stood with comb and scissors
in her hand, fixed to the spot.
'Hi there,' Drew said. 'You're new here
aren't you?' He smiled at her.
The way he used to smile when he played
Doctor Mark Reed in *Ward 7*.
His voice was deep and husky.

'What was he like?'
the other girls asked later.
'What did he say to you?'
'He told me about the play he's in
at the Grand,' Vicky said.
'And he's given me tickets for the show!'
The girls crowded round to look.
Jay clapped his hands.
'The fun's over,' he said. 'Back to work.'

Vicky slipped the tickets into her pocket
with the card Drew had given her.
The card had a message on it.
'ADMIT TWO BACKSTAGE' it said.

On the night of the play she and Mina
sat in the best seats.
At the end, people stood and clapped.
'That was great,' Mina said.
'Wasn't Drew good?
Even better than he is on telly.
Thanks for asking me, Vicky. I can't wait
to meet him. Shall we go backstage?'
Vicky nodded. She was too excited to speak.
She felt glad Mina was with her tonight.
She felt glad that Tony had to work overtime.
He'd only make fun of her for liking Drew.

They went backstage.
They knocked on the door
of Drew's dressing room.
He opened the door himself.
'Come in girls. Have a glass of wine.
I'll just take off my stage make-up.
Then I'll take you to meet
the rest of the cast.'

It was a night to remember.
Vicky felt really great as she walked home.
She thought of Drew's arm around her waist.
The way he'd told the rest of the cast.
'This is the best hairdresser in town.
And by far the prettiest!'

Mina too had been won over by him.
She and Vicky said they would take part
in a fun run Drew was doing.
'It's for charity,' he said. 'In aid of
a new centre for disabled children.
I'm sure two lovely girls like you
will soon find people to sponsor you.'

3

The Fun Run

The day of the fun run was warm and sunny.
Vicky and Mina were there in good time.
They both had a lot of sponsors.
It would be a good advert for the shop.
Jay had got all the clients to sponsor them.
He'd had some outfits made up for them.

Pink running shorts and vests with
'HAIR BY JAY' printed on the front.

'They're a bit bright, these shorts,'
Mina said.
'I know what you mean.' Vicky said,
tugging at them. 'Still it's in a good cause.
And they look really good on you.'
A man from the local paper came over.
He wanted to take a photograph.
'Come on girls,' he said. 'Say cheese, smile.'
He broke off as Drew Denton's car arrived.
'How about a shot with these two babes,
Drew?'
'Of course,' Drew said. He put an arm
round each of them.
'You look fabulous, girls.
I'm glad you could make it.'
It made a good picture.
Drew, with his blond hair,
wearing a gold tracksuit.

Vicky with her red hair and Mina
so dark, in their pink outfits.
'Lovely,' the man said. 'Smile please.'

The runners began to line up.
Men and women of all ages in shorts
and track suits.
Children from scouts and guides.
People were wearing fancy dress:
Batman and Robin,
Rupert Bear. There was even a vampire.
The signal was given. They were off.

A lot of the runners sprinted ahead.
Vicky and Mina stayed with the main group.
The time they took didn't matter.
So long as they did the five miles.
They jogged at a slow pace.
People lined the road at each side.
Vicky saw a group of children near the park.

Some of them were in wheelchairs.
There were adults with them.
As they got nearer she saw
that one of these was Tony.
He was a holding a small boy up
to let him watch the race.

Vicky slowed down.
'I didn't know you were coming,'
she called out to Tony as she passed.
'I didn't know you were!' he shouted back.
Vicky ran on to catch up with Mina.
'Was that Tony?' Mina asked.
Vicky nodded. She found it hard to talk
and run. She wondered why Tony had come.
And who the little boy was.

When they reached the finish Vicky and Mina
fell in a heap, out of breath.

Someone handed them cold drinks.
They went into the tent to get their
sponsor forms signed.
Drew was there looking cool and stylish.
There was a crowd of girls around him.
They were waiting for his autograph.
He came over to them.
'Well done,' he said, kissing them both.
But he held on to Vicky's hand.

Vicky's heart beat faster.
Then she looked over Drew's shoulder.
She was just in time to see Tony
leaving the tent.
'Tony,' she shouted. 'Wait for me.'
She ran across the grass but it was too late.
Tony had gone.

4

A Row With Tony

Vicky didn't see Tony again for a week.

He didn't ring or come round.

She was not going to call him.

Let him sulk if he wanted to.

He'd taken her for granted lately.

She said so to Mina one lunch hour.

'I thought you really liked Tony,' Mina said.
'You always seem to get on well.'
'We do – or rather we did,' Vicky said.
'It's just that he's so down to earth,
so . . . normal. Not romantic at all.
Tony's idea of a good time is a pizza
and a half of shandy.'

'Not like Drew,' Mina said.
'He's got style.'
'We're not talking about Drew,' Vicky said.
'Go on. You know you fancy him!' Mina said.
'Only on the telly,' Vicky said.
But she knew this wasn't true.
She did find Drew very attractive.
Then Tony rang.
'Feel like going for a pizza tonight?'
he asked. Vicky made a face and laughed.
'Yes, OK,' she said. 'See you later.'

'Who was that?' Mina asked.

'The last of the big spenders,' Vicky said.

The evening was not a success.

Vicky chatted about work.

Tony sat, not speaking, not eating much.

'What's up?' Vicky asked.

'Is something wrong?'

'Why didn't you tell me you were going on the fun run?' Tony said at last.

'I thought you'd be working,' Vicky said.

'Drew asked us to help out.'

'Oh it's Drew now, is it?' Tony said.

'Using first names, are we?'

'Don't be silly,' Vicky said.

'What else can I call him?

Anyway, what's he got to do with it?'

'Only that you were all over him
like a rash,' Tony said.
'How do you think I felt – watching
my girlfriend making up to that creep.'
'You don't own me,' Vicky said.
'And Drew's not a creep. He's really nice.
He was telling us how well we had done.'
'Was that all?' Tony snapped.
'It looked more than that to me.
Mind you. He might have got the wrong idea
– with you dressed like that.'
'Dressed like what?' Vicky shouted.
'I was wearing running shorts.'
'Short being the right word,'
Tony shouted back.

'Keep your voice down,' Vicky said.
'People are looking at us.
Jay had the outfits made up for us.

It was all in a good cause.'
'I know it was,' Tony said.
'My nephew goes to that day centre.
I've asked you lots of times to
help out there.
But you've always been too busy.
You're not too busy when Drew Denton
asks you though, are you?'

'Drew does a lot for charity,' Vicky said.
'He enjoys things like the fun run.'
'That's another thing,' Tony said.
'There's no way he could have
done the run in that time.
Not unless he's a world class runner.'
'What are you saying?' Vicky said.
'That he cheated?'
'You're jealous, that's your trouble, Tony.
Jealous of Drew's looks and his fame.'

'Rubbish,' Tony said. 'Me, jealous of
that creep! That'll be the day.
But if you'd rather have him than me.
That's fine by me!'
'Now you're being childish,' Vicky said.
She stood up.
'I'm going home!'
She stomped out to the car.

5

The Party

'So it's all over?' Mina asked on Monday.
'It looks like it,' Vicky said.
'I don't care if I never see Tony again.'
She swept some hair up from the floor
and threw it in the bin.
'Good riddance to bad rubbish!' she said.

The weeks passed, Vicky began
to wonder if she'd been a bit hasty.
She missed Tony. She missed his lifts.
She was standing at the bus stop
one day in the rain. The bus was late.
A car passed, splashing her with water.
A long black car pulled up at the kerb.
The door opened and Drew leaned out.
'Hop in,' he said. 'You're soaked to the skin.
I'll give you a lift.'
Vicky could not believe her luck,
Drew Denton was taking her home.

'I've been hoping to see you,' Drew said.
'The play ends on Saturday.
I want you to come to the last night's party.
Bring that pretty dark haired friend of yours.
It's at my hotel. The Queen's, room 124.'

Vicky was in a daze for the rest of the week.
Who needed a Drew Denton look-alike
when she could have the real thing?
She day-dreamed. She saw herself
arm in arm with Drew at film shows.
Mixing with the stars.
She wondered who she'd meet at the party.

On Saturday she and Mina spent hours
getting ready. Choosing their clothes.
Trying out make-up. Fixing their hair.
They took a taxi to Drew's hotel.
'Come in, girls. Give me your coats.'
Drew showed them into the sitting room.

The room was quite grand, but very untidy.
There were bottles and glasses everywhere.
The ash trays were full.
A plump man with a red face sat on the sofa.

'This is Nev,' Drew said. 'An old friend.'

Nev looked drunk. He patted the sofa.

'Come and sit by me,' he said to Mina.

'What's your name, darling?'

'Mina,' she told him. 'It's a Turkish name.'

'Turkish eh? Are you

going to do some belly dancing for us?'

He patted her knee.

Mina moved away from him.

'Behave yourself Nev,' Drew said.

'Let the girls have a drink first.

What's it be Vicky?'

'White wine and soda, please,' Vicky said.

'Easy on the soda, eh,' Drew said.

He moved towards the table.

He was unsteady on his feet.

Vicky knew he was drunk too.

Drew poured her a glass of wine.

He helped himself to a large scotch.

'Same for you, Mina?' he asked.

'No, just a coke thank you,' Mina said.

'I don't drink.'

'Don't drink? We can't have that.

This is a party. Have a rum in it.'

Mina shook her head. She looked at Vicky.

This wasn't turning out how they thought

it would.

'Are we too early?' Vicky asked.

'When are the others coming?'

'Others? What others?' Nev said.

'You told me this was a private party, Dennis.'

'Dennis?' Vicky said. 'Who's Dennis?'

'My old pal here. Calls himself "Drew" now.

He was always Dennis at school.

Mind you that was years ago.'

Vicky looked at Nev.

He was 40 if he was a day.

She looked at Drew again.

He'd had a lot to drink.

His face looked lined.

She could see the black roots of his hair showing through the blond highlights.

He looked old.

'Yes, he's getting on a bit,' Nev went on.

'That's why he needs me to help him out. You were glad of that lift in the fun run weren't you Den? We couldn't let the poor little kiddies down, could we?'

He started limping round the room.

'Can I have your autograph, Drew.'

Vicky watched in horror as Nev made fun of the disabled children. She waited for Drew to stop him.

Drew laughed. He thought it was funny.

'It's late,' Vicky said, looking at Mina.

'We ought to go. Come on Mina.'

Mina jumped up, glad to escape.

'You can't go yet,' Drew said.

'The party's just warming up.

Have another drink.'

'No thanks,' Vicky said. 'Where's my coat?'

'It's through here,' Drew said.

'In the bedroom.'

Vicky saw her coat on the bed.

She made a grab for it.

But she was too late.

Drew came up behind her.

He pushed her down onto the bed.

'You're not leaving yet,' he said.

Vicky could smell the whisky on his breath

as he tried to kiss her.

Drew pinned her down. He tried again.
Then Vicky lost her temper.
'Get off me,' she shouted.
She twisted away from him.
Drew grabbed at her dress.
Vicky heard the cloth rip.
'That does it!' she said. 'I'm out of here.'
She slapped him hard across the face.
Then ran for the door.

In the other room, Mina was fighting
Nev off on the sofa.
'Come on,' Vicky shouted.
She grabbed Mina's hand and they left.
They ran to the lift.
When they got out at the ground floor,
Vicky saw some work-men there
fitting a new bar.

To her horror she saw that one
of them was Tony.

Vicky couldn't look at him.
He must have seen her.
Seen her torn dress.
Her hair all over the place.
He would guess that she'd been
up in Drew's room.
What would he think of her?
It was bad luck that Tony was working
late, here in this hotel.
Tonight of all nights.

6

Handing over
the Cheque

On Monday, Vicky and Mina were very quiet.
They didn't laugh and joke at all.
At lunch time they talked about the party.
'We were a pair of idiots,' Mina said.
'We fell for the oldest trick in the book.'
'I know,' Vicky said. 'It was my fault.
We were lucky nothing worse happened.'

Jay came up to them.
'The editor of the local paper's
been on the phone,' he said.
'It seems you girls are stars.
They want you to present the cheque
to the day centre on Saturday.
Drew Denton's left town.'
'Thank goodness for that,' Vicky said softly.

The was a big crowd at the day centre.
Children with their mums and dads.
Their teachers and helpers.
The mayor was there. So was the man from
her local paper.
Vicky and Mina went up on the stage.
They held a big cheque in front of them.
Vicky saw Tony at the back of the room.
He looked the same as ever.

Clean and tidy in a checked shirt
and jeans. His hair brushed back.
He looked so normal – and so nice.

Vicky knew now she had been wrong
about Drew.
She had been taken in by his charm.
Tony had been right. Drew was a phoney.
Everything he did was an act.
She wished she could turn the clock back.
Make it up to Tony. But it was too late.

The speeches began.
Vicky and Mina handed over the cheque
to Mrs Kent.
Mrs Kent ran the day centre.
The man from the paper took pictures.
Then Mrs Kent made a speech of thanks.
She thanked the local paper for its support.

She thanked all those who had run.
All those who had given money.
'But I would like to give special thanks,'
she said, 'to our helpers.
They give up time all the year round.
Jim and Mary who do fund raising.
Mrs Ellis who drives the mini bus.
And Tony who does so many odd jobs
for us free of charge.'

Vicky felt her eyes fill with tears.
She knew the truth now.
Drew's charity work was all an act.
He did it for the publicity.
Tony's care was the real thing.

Tea was served. Vicky stayed out of his way.
Tony wouldn't want her now.

She saw him talking to Mina
and longed to be with them.
Then he came over to her.
'Mina's been telling me about the party,'
he said. 'You had a lucky escape.
It's a good job that creep's gone.
He'd have had me to deal with.'
'I'm sorry I ever met him,' Vicky said.
'It was one thing having a silly crush
on an actor.
Meeting the man was different.
You were right. Drew was a phoney.'

'Well I'm sorry for the way I carried on,'
Tony said. 'I guess I was jealous.
And I'm sorry if I took you for granted.
All the overtime I did was for us.
I thought we had a future together.
I suppose it's too late to try again?'
'No,' Vicky said, moving closer to him.
'It's not too late at all.'